Underwater Ca
Coloring Boo

Copyright @ 2024

Underwater Calmenss
Coloring Book

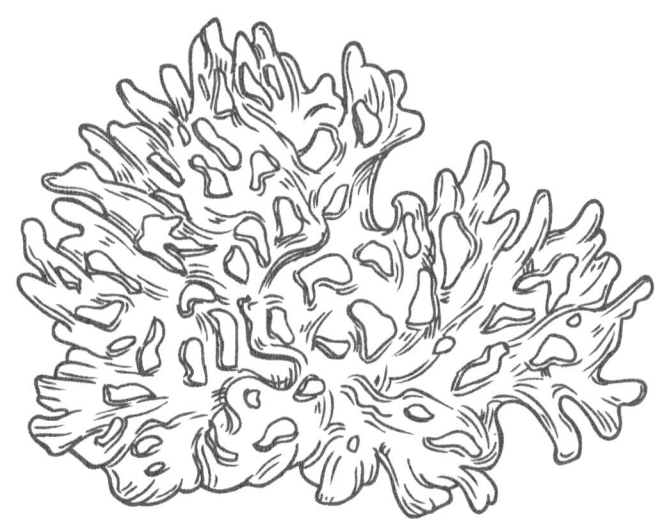

No part of this publication can be reproduced, distributed or transmitted by any means or in any form, including photocopying, recording or other electronical or mechanical methods, without the prior written permission of the publisher, except for brief quotations incorporated in critical reviews and other specific noncommercial uses. Any unathorized replica of this work is prohibited.

Copyright @ 2024

About GregorLia Publishing

Hello there, dear friend!
We here, at GregorLia Publishing, are a family of four. We are passionate about creating a book universe which helps us grown, explore emotions and instill a sense of wonder.

As creators, we feel the need to quiet outside static noise and find ways to better connect with our inner worlds. We wish to enrich life within and around us. Our mission is to be better people than the day before and our books are centered around creating more satisfaction for those who seek them.

Our books are tailored for customers of all ages and skills. We aim to offer joy to tiny humans and adults alike, as we keep in mind the needs of our family members when we design them. They are hand chosen to create storytelling moments, connecting opportunities, tranquil experiences and fulfilling missions.

Allow us to be your guide into this beautiful, bright, clean corner of the world and experience the delight of crafting vibrant masterpieces and cherished moments through our books.

Copyright @ 2024

This book belongs to

_____

_____

Copyright @ 2024

Test Color Page

Copyright @ 2024

Copyright © 2024

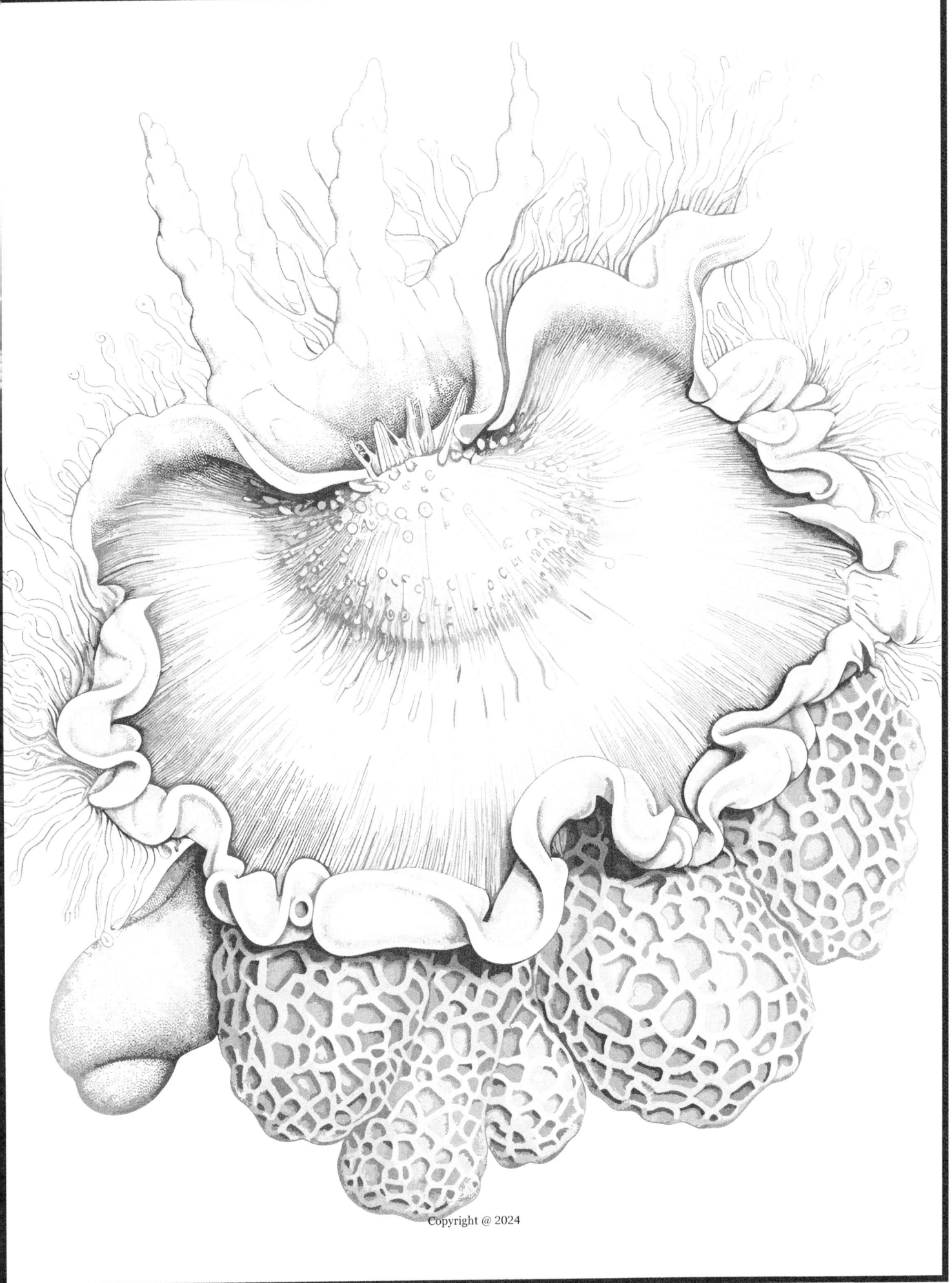

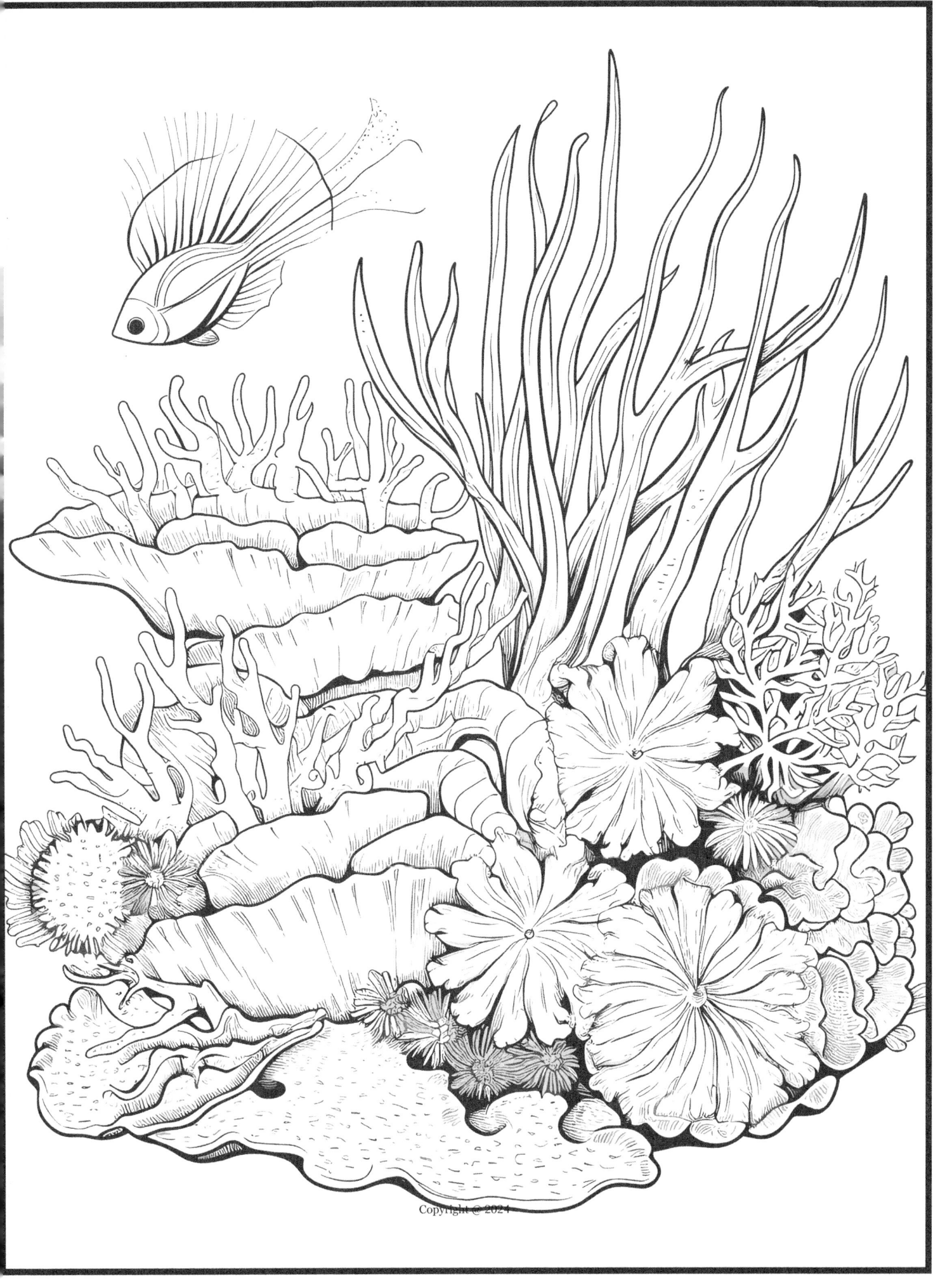

Copyright 2024

Copyright © 2024

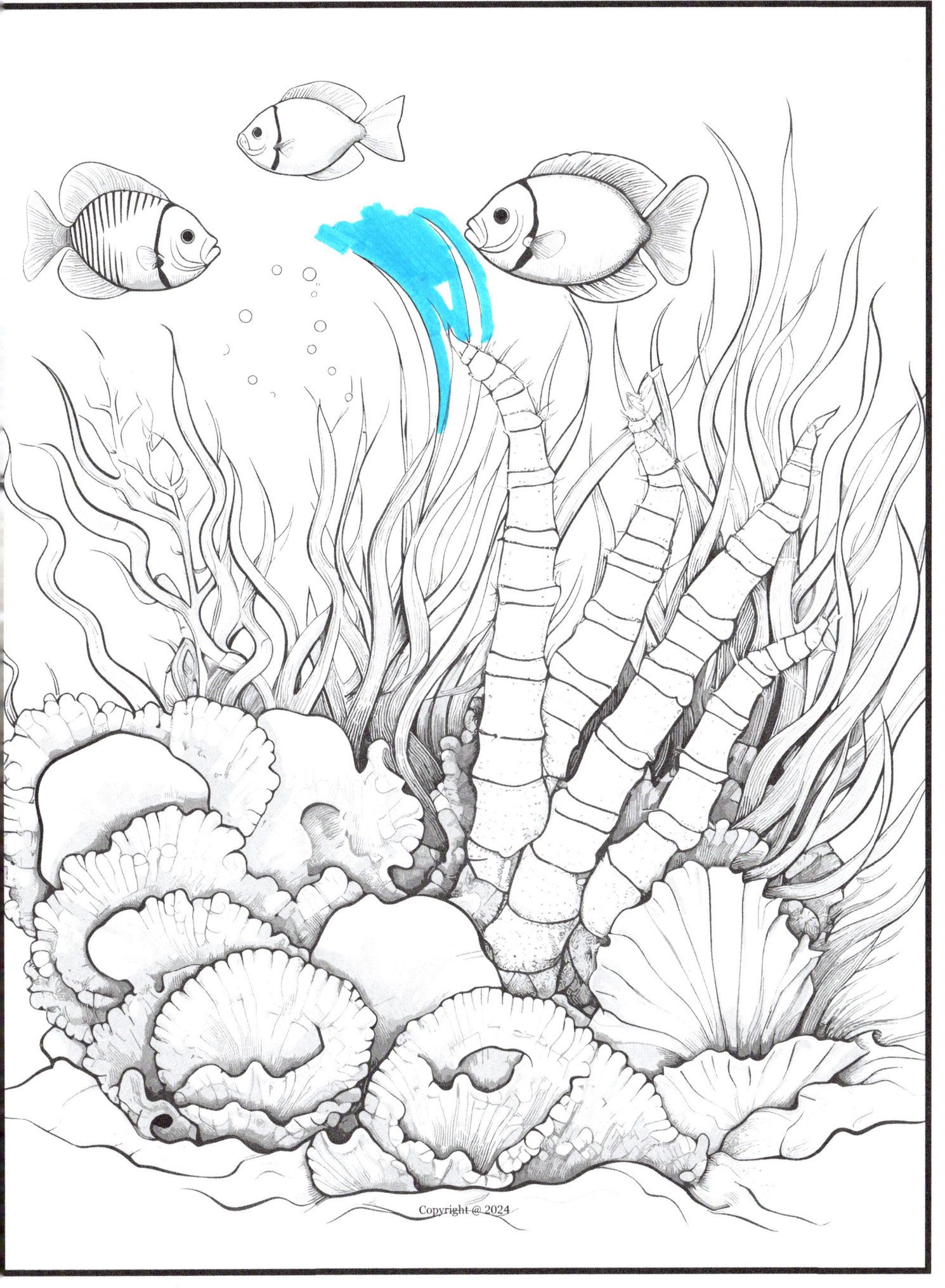

We greatly appreciate the time you took to fill these pages with your vision. It means a lot for us and we hope we made a small difference in your day.

If you have 60 seconds, offering your honest feedback on Amazon would mean the world to us!
It will help the book and it will also help us grow.
We will be very happy to hear about your experience with our book.

To leave your feedback:
1. Open your Camera app
2. Point your mobile device at the QR code bellow
3. The review page will appear in your web browser.

Thank you!

Copyright @ 2024

Copyright © 2024

Copyright © 2024

Copyright © 2024

Copyright © 2024

We greatly appreciate the time you took to fill these pages with your vision. It means a lot for us and we hope we made a small difference in your day.

If you have 60 seconds, offering your honest feedback on Amazon would mean the world to us!
It will help the book and it will also help us grow.
We will be very happy to hear about your experience with our book.

To leave your feedback:
1. Open your Camera app
2. Point your mobile device at the QR code bellow
3. The review page will appear in your web browser.

Thank you!

Copyright @ 2024

Printed in Great Britain
by Amazon